THE
Irresistible
Church SERIES

Doing Life
TOGETHER

Building **COMMUNITY** for **FAMILIES**
AFFECTED BY DISABILITY

by Debbie Lillo

 THE IRRESISTIBLE CHURCH SERIES

Doing Life Together
Print Edition ISBN 978-1-946237-11-8
Kindle Edition ISBN 978-1-946237-12-5
ePUB Edition ISBN 978-1-946237-13-2

Author: Debbie Lillo
Contributing Authors: Sib Charles and Candy Nixon
Collaborators: Stephen Crooks and Jessica Stoop
Editors: Ali Howard and Mike Dobes
Editor in Chief: Eric Jones

Printed in the United States of America.

Produced by The Denzel Agency (www.denzel.org)
Cover and Interior Design: Rob Williams

For information or to order additional print copies of this
and other resources contact:

Joni and Friends International Disability Center
P.O. Box 3333, Agoura Hills, California 91376-3333
Email: churchrelations@joniandfriends.org
Phone: 818-707-5664

Kindle version available at www.irresistiblechurch.org

CONTENTS

"Two are better than one, because they have a good reward for their toil. For if they fall, one will lift up his fellow. But woe to him who is alone when he falls and has not another to lift him up! Again, if two lie together, they keep warm, but how can one keep warm alone? And though a man might prevail against one who is alone, two will withstand him—a threefold cord is not quickly broken."

ECCLESIASTES 4:9-12

Each Sunday morning, families gather to worship and fellowship together at churches across the country. Our souls are nourished by good teaching and Christ-centered community. But what happens when Sunday ends? At what point does church become something more than a Sunday activity and start feeling like family? How do we build the type of community that provides tangible support through life's ups and downs? And how do we do it in such a way that we do not forget to fully include those who might struggle to fit in?

For our friends who have disabilities and their families, simply getting to church on Sunday morning can be a challenge. Making lasting friendships often feels like an unrealistic hope. And while disability affects every member of the family in different ways, it is not uncommon for all of them to experience loneliness and a longing for meaningful friendships. Drained from exhaustion and grief, families affected by disability often find it impossible to pour out the energy necessary to initiate and develop new relationships. Yet, because we are crafted in the image of God, every heart yearns to be loved and known.

Many churches have worked hard to create a Sunday morning environment that welcomes and embraces families affected by disability. This should be celebrated! But the "messiness" of life with a disability extends far beyond Sunday mornings.

This book is a challenge for all of us to step back and recognize that adaptations and programming are important, but they are merely first steps. They allow our friends a place of engagement and access to the church family, but if we are honest, all of us want something deeper than Sunday morning programming. We hunger for quality relationships, for someone with whom we can share the highs and lows of life. We desire to know and be known. This booklet offers practical tools for churches and individuals to help meet daily needs, build community, and alleviate some of the isolation that families affected by disability experience.

This booklet will also help you understand the unique ways that disability affects each member of the family: parents, spouses, siblings, children and grandparents. It also offers practical suggestions on helping every member of the family fully belong. Our prayer is that you find joy in building quality relationships and celebrating as hurting families begin to feel safe, included, understood, and thoughtfully supported. May you be blessed by doing life together!

Understanding the Needs

Alex and his family began attending a church after being invited by a friend. At the time, Alex was 5. Alex has global developmental delays and needed a buddy to be fully included. Their presence at the church prompted the launch of an official disability ministry. Their family has thrived at the church for nearly 15 years now. Mom and Dad have made quality friendships and have served in several capacities. Alex and his two siblings have grown up with this church family. Recently, one of Alex's brothers declared his desire to follow Christ and was baptized. As the leadership team celebrated his baptism, the whole church was struck anew that disability ministry is indeed a whole-family ministry.

Every family affected by disability is unique, and every member of each family is affected uniquely. To understand the challenges faced by the families you serve, it helps to consider a broader view. Luke 14:21b, 23 – *"Go out quickly to the streets and lanes of the city, and bring in the poor and crippled and blind and lame... and compel people to come in, that my house may be filled."*

When a family experiences disability, life is drastically altered. Dreams are turned upside down. For some, disability arrives during pregnancy when diagnostic exams indicate a baby is not developing typically. Other families face disability at birth, or in the preschool years. For others, it is caused by an illness or accident later in life. Regardless of how and when disability occurs, it results in challenging decisions as family members are thrown quickly into advocacy roles they had not prepared for. Grief over a disability is as real as grief over a death. It follows the same stages of grief as described so well by Elisabeth Kübler-Ross, although the stages are not as chronological and it is chronic. For example, when a young mother who has a daughter with Down syndrome is invited to the birthday party of her daughter's typical peer, she might be thrown back to the initial stages of grief and begin the cycle anew. The grief experienced by a special needs parent is often coupled by guilt because the parent feels they should not grieve—believing that grief somehow means they do not love their child deeply enough.

Families often begin to fear rejection when they have been repeatedly told that their family member with a disability doesn't belong. When, for example, parents of a young child with autism are told that the community programs are not equipped to welcome their child, or that they cannot attend library story time, they become apprehensive about venturing out to try other social activities. Every time parents hear, "I'm sorry, we cannot accommodate..." it is a heart-breaking rejection. Over and over, families affected by disability feel rejected in direct or subtle ways. It is not unusual for families to feel like a rejection from church is somehow a rejection from God. Our desire is to help families affected by disability understand the truth that God will never leave them or forsake them. In this section of the book, let's take a look at how each member of the family might process their experience with disability and why they may struggle with isolation.

Parents and Caregivers

Parents and caregivers spend massive amounts of energy trying to juggle all their responsibilities while loving their family as best they can. Many daily chores that take a typical family a few minutes to complete can take a family affected by disability hours to accomplish. A family member with autism might find it extremely challenging to leave the comfort of their pajamas to dress, eat breakfast, and transition to the car each morning. An adult family member with limited mobility will need to be transferred, bathed, and fed before his family can leave the house. Medications need to be monitored. New therapies need to be researched and scheduled. The schedules of typical siblings need to be aligned with doctor appointments, therapy appointments, and education consultation appointments. At bedtime, many of the morning challenges are repeated. When both parents are home, they may tag-team the work, but by the end of the day there is rarely time to breathe, let alone talk. It should be no surprise that families affected by disability tend to be exhausted, and they often lack the energy to develop outside relationships. They may grieve the future they had once imagined.

When these families venture out into the community, they often find a hostile reception. Parents of children with special needs tire of unsolicited advice and judgment, often choosing to stay home rather than experience it. While the world is slowly becoming more accepting of individuals with disabilities, families often still receive fearful stares and judgmental comments. If their children exhibit behavioral challenges in public, people who observe might respond by somehow indicating that the parents are spoiling their child or failing as parents. This is especially challenging for parents of children with disabilities that are not outwardly visible. These children are regularly seen as poorly behaved or uneducated. Families may fear judgment—either because a stressed house is not usually a tidy house or because they feel judgment over their parenting skills. As a result, parents often retreat, feeling that isolation is a safer alternative. Isolation can become chronic—the more a family chooses not to participate, the harder and more fearful it becomes to reach out. The more isolated the family, the easier it is for the church to ignore the need. Isolation is magnified because life is so busy and moves at such a quick pace. Sib Charles, co-author of this book and wife to a wonderful husband who is a quadriplegic, noted, "Families affected by disability cannot keep up with the quick pace. We're so busy running that we don't see it. We start to withdraw more and more as our pace of life differs drastically from others." Many of these families feel they do not fit into the typical world. In light of that, the church must try to step into their world.

Single parents are especially vulnerable to isolation. They spend many hours caregiving without other adults to provide perspective and help. It is often challenging to keep up with outside friendships or even know what is happening in the lives of friends. It can be harder for a single parent to keep up with daily chores, so they might be embarrassed to invite others in. Finances are generally tighter with only one income, and they may struggle seeing their children with fewer "things" than their peers. Juggling the activities of multiple children is much more challenging without a spouse. The combination of these factors can leave single parents feeling exceptionally isolated.

Most parents and caregivers know they need community, and they desire to have quality relationships. They want the time to think and wrestle with God over the big questions that suffering produces—but they are tired. Once families feel rejected from community activities, they grow increasingly hesitant to risk rejection from the church.

Social media is filled with everyone posting all the things they do—exciting things and even ordinary things that are sometimes simply not possible for many special needs families. It can be challenging to watch other children maturing typically while their beloved child struggles to reach milestones. In an effort to avoid fruitless jealousy and heartache, it is easy to choose isolation and pull away even more.

Parents and caregivers will all respond to trying circumstances differently. Some will be able to manage the needs they face in a way that is healthy, while many others will be tempted to retreat and withdraw. The body of Christ has a unique opportunity to love families facing hardship by entering their world and inviting them into authentic friendships.

Caregivers of Spouses with Disabilities

Caregivers of spouses with disabilities face unique and relentless challenges. For example, there is an elderly woman at a local church in Virginia who shared with us her struggle to care for her husband who battles Alzheimer's disease. With tears in her eyes, she confessed that she was exhausted and lonely but would not know how to have someone help her. Most of her day is spent trying to prevent things from happening: answering the phone before her husband does so that he doesn't give out confidential information; deleting emails before he sees them so that he doesn't order items on the internet; safeguarding her husband from physical injury. She also shared with us her deep grief over the loss of spiritual encouragement that she used to share with her husband. At this point, he is no longer able to share scripture with her and pray with her. She has such a hunger for other women to surround her to encourage her heart spiritually.

While deeply committed to loving their spouse, the caregiving spouse can become exhausted and strained by what is often an uneven burden in parenting and providing for the family. When the disability makes it challenging for one spouse to work, the other spouse becomes the primary breadwinner. If driving is a challenge, the caregiving spouse then becomes the errand runner and transportation provider for all family members. The caregiver essentially has three full-time jobs: employment, keeping up with household chores, and caregiving. One caregiver described it as "sometimes feeling like you have a third person in your marriage—the disability." It can be challenging to make nurturing the marriage a priority. The demands of caregiving leave little time for fun, spontaneity, and energy to see the spouse as one's lover. Vacations can be limited and challenging.

Caregivers often need encouragement to seek help from attendants so that they can recharge and rest. There are times when the caregiver or spouse struggles to accept their need for assistance. Feelings of guilt can overwhelm the caregiver. Thoughts can scream in their heads, saying, *I should be able to do all of this on my own! This is my responsibility!* This is where the church can step in and offer help by meeting some of the practical needs. This could include providing transportation; offering to do some light housekeeping, yard care, and/or house repairs; or spending time with the spouse who has the disability to give the able-bodied spouse some self-care time. The spouse with the disability may also hesitate to accept care from others because they are struggling with the reality of their own limitations. Saying, "If you need anything, give me a call," to a caregiver will likely never result in a phone call. But if you offer a practical and specific act of care, then they will most likely accept the offer with gratitude. As each family's needs are unique, caring for them cannot be done in a one-size-fits-all approach; there must be flexibility based on the situation.

When a spouse has a disability, it is very difficult to find other couples who share a similar life journey. When talking about the struggles related to the physical and emotional challenges of intimacy, it is hard to be authentic with friends who do not have a spouse with a disability. Infertility is a significant struggle for many couples where one spouse has a disability. The struggle with infertility, as well as anxiety over potential struggles that result from parenting with a spouse who has a disability, can have a significant effect on the marriage. Children, household duties and work keep most couples busier than they want to be; how much more is this true for couples who must also consider the responsibilities of caregiving? It can also be a challenge to find ways for the parent with the disability to feel fulfilled in the parenting role. Even if you don't fully relate or understand, the gift of listening without judgment to a couple who is living this journey is a gift beyond words. They need a safe, Christ-centered environment to share their struggles.

While isolation can certainly be an issue for caregivers and their spouse with a disability, Christ can supply their every need—just as in any other marriage. Even in the midst of these challenges, well-supported caregivers and their spouses can live full lives, and disabled parents can have fun and vibrant relationships with their children.

Parents Caregiving Together

Marriages affected by disability experience incredible strain and often do not survive. Mothers are more likely than fathers to take on the caregiving responsibility, but whoever assumes this role is often forced to give up all or part of their role in the work world. This has financial implications and can also affect the self-image and morale of that parent. Parents who formerly held a balance of time at home and outside the home suddenly find themselves focusing most of their attention caring for the family member with disabilities. There is little time to focus on household duties or to invest in the marriage relationship. Resentment can build on both sides. One caregiving father shared with us, "I feel like my wife is having an affair—with my child. We share a bed but she only focuses on our child."

Exhaustion can lead to jealousy, and jealousy can appear in many different shades for many reasons. A homebound spouse may be jealous of the spouse who can work outside the home. A couple living with disability in their family might be jealous of friends who lead typical lives, go on vacations, and have easy date nights. It is exceptionally challenging to combat jealousy or communicate needs when both parents are running on fumes and the majority of their time together is spent meeting the needs of their children. Left unchecked, jealousy can lead to resentment and a host of other negative emotions. Unless both parents find avenues of self-care, exhaustion can erode their marriage.

It can be a challenge for caregiving couples to have quality time together—time to talk, process, and enjoy each other. They also lack time as individuals to find respite and refuel. Time is one of the greatest enemies of a marriage impacted by special needs.

Whether spoken or unspoken, parents often find themselves blaming their partner for their new reality. In some cases, there are true genetic links to the disability, but often there are unspoken theories about why the disability occurred. Many cultures add a strong message of guilt and blame on parents in this difficult context—believing that in some way one or both parents brought the disability upon the family. Blame and shame can deal a weighty blow on even the healthiest of marriages.

It is probably not a surprising statement to say that husbands and wives process stress differently. Men and women are wired uniquely by God and that balance often contributes toward the making of extremely healthy relationships. But when faced with challenging situations, husbands and wives tend to have contrasting responses. One may jump into advocacy and caregiving while the other withdraws and tries to fix what's broken. Without time to debrief and talk through the differences, resentment can build over how the other spouse is choosing to respond.

Isolation can distort the couple's perspective. They might feel they are alone, not seeing the "normalcy" of their experience, because they do not have the opportunity to observe other marriages faced with the same challenges or seek tools for improving their marriage. Weaknesses and bad habits that existed in the marriage relationship are magnified by disability. Rather than finding a new normal, one or both spouses may begin to make choices that are destructive to the marriage.

Efforts to break isolation can be marriage-saving. Supporting each spouse individually as well as together allows a couple the time and effort to process their circumstances and respond in a way that is glorifying to God.

Typical Siblings

Typical siblings experience unique embarrassment and confusion that can lead to feelings of disconnectedness. They generally hold a deep love for their sibling with a disability and yet yearn for a "normal" family experience, feeling as though no one understands or appreciates their daily challenges. While some siblings choose to use their brother or sister as a litmus test for potential significant others, others choose not to risk rejection and avoid bringing friends or potential significant others home. Siblings are often mature for their age because they experience responsibilities that most of their peers do not. They often step in to help around the house and aid with their sibling's care. Their parents frequently struggle to meet all their needs or celebrate their accomplishments because their energy is spent focusing on the sibling with greater needs.

Without intentional nurturing and care, typical siblings can get buried in anger and resentment. Without proper understanding, they might fear they caused their sibling's disability or wonder if they will catch it. They often worry about the future or about the financial strain they observe. They might feel an extreme sense of responsibility to be the easy or good child, and they might struggle with guilt over their feelings of embarrassment or accomplishment. Their grief often mirrors that of their parents, but young siblings rarely have the skills or support to process grief in a healthy way.

Most parents desire to support their typical children well, but they are often overwhelmed. It sometimes helps to have a trusted adult friend who can intentionally mentor typical siblings, helping them find their own place, and celebrating them for who they are separate from their unique family life. As the body of Christ, we should try to celebrate each member of our congregation, inviting them to participate and be heard.

Extended Family

Extended family often feel pushed aside when a family unit experiences disability. Once-expressive adult children are now struggling to keep their heads above water and might not want "helpful" input from Mom or Dad. Being kept at arm's length can be excruciatingly painful for grandparents, aunts and uncles who would do anything to alleviate the pain their loved ones are feeling. In many cultures, these relationships are further strained by feelings of shame and guilt, or by strong feelings of judgment.

If the immediate family unit is able to function in a way that is sustainable and healthy, extended family relationships will also be able to grow. When the church supports family members who are immediately affected, we are also supporting the extended family.

Every member of a family affected by disability can and probably will experience overwhelming stressors. Because disability affects every member of the family, friendship and belonging challenges are felt strongly by the parents, the caregivers, the siblings, the extended family, and the individual who has the disability.

The church has the honor of being God's hands and feet to a hurting world. Proverbs 31:8 tells us to speak up for those who cannot speak for themselves. Families affected by disability are often weary and feel unable to articulate their needs. As Joni Eareckson Tada often says, "God allows disability so that his church can learn compassion." Families facing chronic illness or disability often lack the energy to navigate the world of church fellowship, yet the church is the very best place for hurting and broken people to come and be encouraged. We recognize that it can sometimes be overwhelming and paralyzing to consider the scope of their need; this is why the rest of this book is filled with practical and scalable ways that your church can partner with these families to answer the following questions:

- How do I combat isolation?
- I have real, practical needs, but how do I ask for help?
- How do I build community?
- Where is God in all of this, and how do I find comfort from God?

Using these questions as our outline, let's take a look at tangible ways a church might support these specific needs. Within each of the following sections, if you find yourself wanting further information, we invite you to check out the online appendices associated with this book.

Combatting Isolation

Based purely on external appearances, the Johnson family looks like a "typical" American family. But if you took a closer look, you would learn that Frank struggles with ever-progressive multiple sclerosis. Kate has many medical issues of her own, and all three of their children have chronic autoimmune diseases that constantly keep them on the verge of illness and hospitalization. For many years they stayed as active as they could, but over time they had to spend more time at home because of their limited energy to engage with other families. This grew to be a significant problem; they felt isolated but stuck. Recently they found two other couples with similar struggles. Together these families have made a huge—and challenging—commitment to meet weekly for dinner. Even if someone cannot come, the rest still meet. In this environment, they understand and welcome the messiness of one another's lives. In the brief time since they began this weekly dinner, Frank and Kate have already seen huge gains in their mental outlook and encouragement.

There are families like the Johnsons all around us, but not all of them are able to find community as easily. How can the local church make it easier for families like this to step out of isolation? Isolation is at the core of nearly every stressor faced by families affected by disability; because of this, it is one of the core issues we address in this book. Being isolated means not having contact with people outside of the family, and it can lead to feeling like there is no place to belong. It is an excruciatingly painful feeling.

Keeping up with the challenges that come from disability can make families so busy that they often don't see isolation coming. Their lives are so full and their hearts so exhausted that they cannot see the need until it is chronic. Once the need is recognized, it comes with heartbreak and pain. Some families are so weary from caregiving that finding a solution to their isolation feels overwhelming. As we previously noted, their isolation may come in part from the fear of rejection or from unsolicited advice. They may be overwhelmed and fearful of letting others see the chaos of their lives. Some may even fear their own feelings of jealousy that arise if they get too close to peers with fewer struggles. If they are single, their isolation is magnified by the added burdens of parenting without a partner to share the load or give perspective. And siblings experience their own unique isolation as they live lives that are often very different from their peers.

Zachary White, author at The Caregiver Network, wrote a blog about caregiving titled "Inside Out." In this article, he compels us to imagine looking out the window of the bedroom where he sat caring for his ailing mother. He could see everyone passing by, but they did not even glance his way. He yearned for someone to notice him. But they were busy living their lives and could not see his isolation and pain. He writes, "For caregivers, our inside-out view of the world can make us feel invisible, alone, isolated and, yes, like outsiders."[1]

A logical first step in combatting isolation is to be certain that we have opened the doors of our churches and removed all barriers. Even if a family affected by disability has the energy and courage to engage in the life of a church, they will be unable to do so if the church is not accessible. If you are not sure whether your facilities are accessible, we encourage you to check out the online appendices for this book where you will find an accessibility checklist.⦿ This checklist was built to help churches consider what it takes to create environments where individuals with disabilities can fully participate. If your facilities do not allow individuals with disabilities to engage in the life of the body, all your efforts toward inclusion will be in vain. However, beyond the physical church building, it is also important to consider if the teaching and heart of your church are accessible. Adapting curriculum⦿ and disability awareness training for your volunteers⦿ can make a massive difference in how comfortable families feel attending your church.

Once you have removed barriers to physical inclusion, you can begin to consider the type of support a family affected by disability would need in order to fully belong. Trained buddies⦿ can come alongside families at church events, allowing them to participate in ways that would have otherwise been out of the question. Consider contacting families impacted by disability directly and asking them what kind of activities they would feel comfortable attending;

⦿ This symbol indicates that there are supplemental resources that correspond with this topic at http://irresistiblechurch.org/library/

then make your plans accordingly. If possible, church activities should be held in locations that are physically accessible and free from sensory triggers.

We spoke with a small church in Pennsylvania that learned that one of their families felt uncomfortable joining church family potlucks because the family took up a great deal of space at the table and their children's behavior might be challenging. Wanting the family to feel welcome, the church began to set aside a large square table for them with a sign that read "Reserved." It was a small effort, but it was one that was felt deeply by the family. The mother of this family wrote, "At first it felt a little weird, but not anymore! It is a *huge* relief to just pull right in and get down to the business of dinner! Tonight, I looked at that sign and thought, *I am so grateful!* This, for us, was disability ministry done better. It moved beyond Sunday mornings and made us feel welcome around the table later in the work week. It says, 'We want you here; we expect you here.' Kudos to our church family and thanks for making room for us at the Banquet Table (Luke 14:15-24)."

Combatting isolation is not necessarily complicated, but it does take time and effort. The implications, however, are life-changing!

RECAP:
Tangible Steps a Church Might Take to Combat Isolation

1. Assess access—physical access, access to the gospel, and attitudinal access.
2. Intentionally welcome and provide support at all family activities.
3. Train buddies who are available not only for Sunday mornings but also for weekday and special activities.
4. Ask families impacted by disability for guidance and suggestions.

Note
1. https://thecaregivernetwork.ca/inside/

Meeting
Practical Needs

The church is generally quick to step up when someone gets sick or passes away. We deliver meals, meet practical needs, and offer encouragement. But what happens when the meal train slows down and people stop visiting? Grief and disability both offer a relentless reality that must be faced day after day.

Families affected by disabilities have both short-term needs and long-term needs. Some families can manage these needs, while others will benefit from practical help. Short-term care may include supporting the family when the person affected by disability faces surgery or requires special advocacy at school. It might also include urgent help around the house or transportation crises. Long-term care considers the day-in, day-out stressors that don't go away. It involves both small acts of kindness that will relieve some of that pressure as well as building management systems that provide support and protection from fatigue. Let's take a look at tools and suggestions that can help meet urgent, short-term needs; we will also address caring for chronic needs that can wear families down and lead to despair.

Before you consider caring for the needs of the families in your ministry, it is important to remember that when you engage in caretaking, you are entering the private lives of families. Some families will be so eager to receive your help that they will share freely the confidential details of their lives. Other families will be more reserved and cautious in sharing their personal details. Regardless of how comfortable each family is with sharing, it is important that we honor their privacy and proceed according to their leading. Allow them to set the tone for what kind of help they want as well as how much help they want. As you focus on the needs that might be met, remember that these families are far more than the disability or challenges they face. Your goals should include building friendships and celebrating life with them. Your conversations with the family should not center solely on the disability at hand. Caregivers from all ages and stages of life have shared with us that they grow weary of always talking about and updating people on their family's disability-related struggles. They desire to be celebrated for who they are, apart from the disability.

Meeting practical needs has three primary components: (1) knowing what to say, (2) knowing what to do, and (3) creating a system for the ongoing care of the family.

Knowing What to Say

It can be challenging to know what to say when you are trying to support a friend in need. Many a well-meaning friend has stumbled for words and unintentionally said something hurtful to their friend in pain. Henry Nouwen offers wonderful advice on this topic in his book *Out of Solitude*: "A friend who can be silent with us in a moment of despair or confusion, who can stay with us in an hour of grief and bereavement, who can tolerate not knowing...not healing, not curing...that is a friend who cares."

Sometimes it is best to just sit with your friend and say nothing at all. It can be challenging to sit beside a hurting friend without offering words of encouragement or advice. We exhort you to step beyond that discomfort and see how both you and your friend will be blessed. Your presence, your warmth, and your love will minister deeply. Sometimes your presence may actually be more meaningful than any words you could share.

Before offering any words of comfort, it is important to earn the right to speak. Encouragement from someone you love is far more meaningful than encouragement from an acquaintance. Once you have gained that relationship and feel comfortable approaching your friend, we would suggest avoiding phrases that imply that you understand your friend's pain. Only your friend can truly understand the difficulty of their situation. Saying things like, "I know exactly what you feel..." can cause more pain and frustration than support. It is better to use a catch-phrase of support such as "I'm so sorry you are hurting" or "I'm here to pray for and support you however I can."

It can also be wise to avoid unsolicited biblical platitudes like the following phrases: *God wouldn't give you more than you can handle; In all things God works for good; God knows you're the perfect mother for Joey.* These insights are not helpful and can even be destructive in the midst of pain. Diane Kim is an author, speaker, and mother of two sons, one of whom has autism. She often summarizes this concept when she speaks, saying:

As I grieved the death of my Idealized Child, well-meaning church friends attempted to console with encouraging words and Bible verses,

"God won't give you anything you can't handle."
"Special needs children are a blessing!"
"Trust God. He is good!"

Just stop. Please. In the face of *"Severely disabled. Mentally retarded. Prognosis unknown,"* how is disability a blessing? How is God still good? Our son was cognitively disabled; and I was spiritually crippled. That single piece of paper diagnosing my son severed all existing connections between my head and heart. Any pre-existing conditions, convictions and even feelings went numb as disillusionment and spiritual death hovered near. My faith was flat-lining. We *both* required urgent and intensive intervention.[1]

Several years ago, Susan Silk and Barry Goldman wrote an insightful article about unsolicited advice and emotion in the *Los Angeles Times*.[2] They presented a circle surrounded by several other circles. They asked the reader to imagine that in the very center of the innermost circle is a person experiencing pain. The next ring would be that individual's immediate family, those who are also indirectly experiencing the pain. Friends, caregivers, medical and therapy support providers, and extended family populate the remaining circles depending on how far each person is from the crisis itself. Silk and Goldman titled this the "Comfort in. Dump out" model. They suggest that everyone in the outer circles should only offer words of comfort to the people in the center of the rings. They should not verbally analyze or openly complain about the situation. Only those in the center can "dump" negative words or offer suggestions. Those in the center of the rings might ask for advice and even research, but those in the outer rings should only contribute those things by invitation.

It can be challenging to support a friend without offering advice or commentary. Principles like the one presented in the *Los Angeles Times* article can be extremely helpful guidelines as we navigate these difficult circumstances. Doing life together with sensitivity allows us to help our friend move through a trying time feeling loved and supported without adding challenges or frustrations. It can also open the door to long-term relationship and healing.

Knowing What to Do

The rewarding and creative part of supporting our friends as they experience pain and disability comes in the doing. There are many creative ways to walk alongside your friend and make his or her burden more bearable. The sky is the limit and the potential is endless! We don't necessarily need to do weighty things; we just need to listen to the need of our friend and listen to the Holy Spirit's still, small voice. We have included an online resource that summarizes some of the ways we've seen churches meet practical needs with thoughtful joy.꣸ But before you read that list, challenge yourself to think about what your friend loves, what day-to-day tasks would be hard or impossible for them to do, what siblings in the family might be feeling put aside because of the disability, and what their caregivers might simply enjoy. Try to think beyond the urgent needs regarding things they might want. Even though it might not be the most practical help, sometimes the most soothing balm to a hurting soul is to restore a sense of normalcy by doing the things your friend enjoys—getting a pedicure or spending time outside in the sun, for example. Allowing your friend to be heard is a gift of great value; taking time to listen as they process and understand what they really need will validate them and allow you to serve them more effectively.

As we previously mentioned, try not to offer vague assistance by saying things like "What can I do to help you?" or "If you need anything, call me." As well meaning as those questions may be, they can be overwhelming to a family that is drowning in a challenging situation. Be specific in your offer, such as "I'll be going to the grocery store in 30 minutes just down the street from your house. Can I pick up some fresh fruit and milk for you?" or "It's spring, and I know how much you enjoy your garden. I'd love to come by on Saturday morning and plant some tulip bulbs for you." By phrasing your assistance in this way, it gently encourages your friend to receive your care while offering specific and needed support.

Debbie Lillo, co-author of this book and a long-time disability advocate, recently saw this concept played out in her own life when a friend texted her to let her know that their 16-year-old son with autism was heading to the PICU. Debbie shared, "My first attempt at support was to say, 'Would you like prayerful company while you sit by his side?' She appreciated my offer, but it sounded like work to her. A bit later I texted her, 'The ministry leader at your church and I were thinking we'd bring by some snacks to get you through the night. We could sit with your other son when you talk to the doctor.' She quickly asked, 'What time can you be here?!'"

After talking with your friend and their family, it may be clear that they do not have the time or energy to keep up with yard work or with household chores. You might offer to pick up their car and get it washed. There may be specific house or car-maintenance needs that someone in the church has the skills and time to meet. Someone might learn the physical care needs of the family member with a disability in order to provide respite for the caregivers. Someone else may be able to provide transportation for typical siblings to special events or sports practices. You might also consider helping a child, who could not on their own, create a Mother's Day or Father's Day card, or you could keep track of birthdays in the family and help celebrate them in a special way.

A church in North Carolina decided to purchase a small artificial Christmas tree for each child with a disability in their congregation. Each family filled out tags that hung on their tree as ornaments, and each tag described an opportunity to spend time with their child. For example, tags on one tree read: Take Rick to a minor league baseball game; Join our family for game night; Cheer Rick on at Miracle League baseball; Ride bikes with Rick in our neighborhood. A tree was placed in every adult Sunday School class and that class adopted that family for the next year. Each class member could pick the activity he or she wanted to complete. It was amazing to see how many friendships and beautiful memories were born out of this Christmas activity!

When someone is in the hospital, consider creating a care package for the family that includes snacks, pampering items, and reading or craft items. You might provide rides, meals, or sleepovers for the siblings left behind. Offering to pick up prescriptions or toiletries or doing a load of laundry while the parents sit at the hospital can be very helpful. For the family member with the medical needs, you could create an encouragement basket of hopeful and fun items to keep their spirits up while they are in the hospital.

As you get to know the families in your congregation, you will discover creative ways to support them. While we have shared with you a handful of ideas, we encourage you to use these suggestions as a launchpad to brainstorm new ideas. Consider the talents and resources of your church family as you evaluate the needs of the families you are serving. You will find the possibilities to be endless!

Knowing How to Organize

When it became clear that little Yoki's illness was terminal, church friends wanted to support his family but did not know how. A close friend of the family realized that Yoki's mom was discouraged by telling the story over and over again; she was too tired to even consider what kind of support her family needed. Her faithful friend stepped into the role of point-person for Yoki's family—like a care coordinator or chief of staff to funnel and route all communications and offers of help that came in from their different circles of friends and family. She communicated regularly with Yoki's family and asked honest "what helps, what doesn't help" questions. She offered practical tips about visitations and meal preferences to anyone wanting to visit the family. This allowed the family space to treasure Yoki's last months of life and allowed the community to support them in creative and truly useful ways during his illness and beyond.

Supporting families in need can be overwhelming, especially if the need is chronic and the care team is small. It can also be confusing because well-meant gestures are sometimes not well received. But the act of supporting one another in times of need is the true essence of living life together, and the reward is great. Jill Lynn Buteyn and Kara Tippetts's touching and practical book, *Just Show Up*, offers amazing encouragement and advice on this subject. Kara was a young mom with small children when she learned she was dying, and her church learned how to walk with her in her final days. This experience changed their church and the way they now live as a family of believers in the wake of Kara's death. This book offers intimate insight into building deep relationships and creating community through challenging times. Kara explained it well in the introduction: "There is so much power in showing up, humble power in saying, 'I'm here. I may not have all of the answers, but I'm here.'"[3] Intentional support can make all the difference for a family walking through illness or loss of a loved one; distributing responsibilities in a healthy manner allows you to prioritize the care that is most needed while providing checks and balances to avoid co-dependency or burnout.

As you endeavor to support a family facing hardship, consider appointing someone who the family trusts and is comfortable with to act as the point of communication with everyone outside the family. As in Yoki's story, this allows the family to be honest and direct about what kind of help they need or want without the awkwardness of having to ask, decline, or coordinate it themselves. There are several excellent online tools for communicating food and support needs.⌘ Kara and Jill came up with a system to tell people dropping off food whether they should ring the doorbell as Kara was often too weak or too ill to receive visitors. They posted a chalkboard by the front door, and Jill made sure it was kept up to date with messages for anyone coming to drop off food or to visit. It let them know if they should ring the bell and gave instructions to leave food in the ice chest by the door if the family was not up to seeing visitors.

For chronic care, consider creating a team of people to support each area of that family's life: food, rides and care for siblings, hospital visit support, errand support, and whatever specific categories the family may need. Each member of this team can organize other friends to help them, but they should report to the one person who is communicating directly with the family.

As your care extends beyond a single family who needs help for a specific short-term need, we highly encourage you to establish an intentional and well-structured system of care. Establishing such a system will allow your church body to care not only for families impacted by disability, but also for other church family members in need. The Covenant Care Ministry at the Reformed Presbyterian Church of Ephrata, Pennsylvania, gives us a wonderful example of what this might look like. For every family in need, a group of church members agree to walk alongside the family by providing support through prayer and tangible help. They define their Covenant Care groups as "a covenantal relationship between a family in exceptionally difficult circumstances (usually not of their own making) and a small group of church members who commit to assisting the family in the meeting of legitimate needs. Covenant Care is a burden-bearing ministry in a very biblically bounded sense." Your church may find that Bible study or community groups are willing to offer care, or perhaps new groups should be formed to coordinate prayer, fellowship, advocacy, and care. Having an intentional system helps meet the needs of families facing hardship while offering clear guidelines to those who are helping. We have provided tips for creating a covenant care ministry in the online resources for this book.❧

Any structured care system should include frequent evaluation❧ and intentional support for the health of the support teams. Caregiving can be exhausting, and overwhelmed families can sometimes hope for or expect things from a well-meaning support system that are beyond their capabilities. Provide biblical counseling for the families you support as well as for your support team as needed. Your evaluation should include guidelines for maintaining healthy boundaries and avoiding co-dependency. You and your support team should never allow your own families to suffer while helping another family.

Supporting in a healthy manner can be particularly challenging when long-term care for a chronic illness or disability is necessary. While practical support can help a family get back on their feet or make it through a crisis season, some families will need continuing support for things they will never be able to do on their own. Ongoing emotional support can be incredibly important for families facing chronic disability or the loss of a loved one. Brad Mortensen, a pastor involved with disability ministry, suggests that the care team overseers continue to remind the team—and the families—that only God can ultimately provide our needs. While this doesn't diminish the need for practical help, it does encourage everyone involved to look first to Christ, and it allows caregivers to simply be seen as his hands and feet. If the family begins to think of the support team as the "savior," the relationship is no longer healthy. As soon as the supporters think of themselves as indispensable, the relationship is equally unhealthy. Families need practical care, but it must always be paired with loving spiritual nourishment; we will talk about spiritually supporting families impacted by disability later in this book.

Emily Colson, author of *Dancing with Max*, turned to her church family for help when her son Max aged out of the school system. "Autism," Emily explained to the support team she gathered, "is a team sport." Emily assembled what she called her Go2 Team—a group of people who loved both Emily and Max on their best and worst days. She made it clear to them that she was not asking them to do her work for her, let her off the hook on her responsibilities, provide ongoing care, or make decisions for her. Instead, she asked this group of church family members to be the team she could approach when she faced a problem too big for her to handle alone, to provide back-up care for Max, to step in during emergencies, and to provide friendship when she was exhausted or overwhelmed. This Go2 Team has proven to be a healthy and successful caregiving model for Emily and has ensured that a circle of trusted adults are surrounding Max as he navigates young adulthood.

When we thoughtfully work together to meet one another's needs, we express God's love in a unique way. Supporting caregivers will open the door for deeper friendships, meet their practical needs, and allow us to experience the joy of their friendship. Through the process of caregiving, we have much to learn from the families that we serve while we help them find a sustainable rhythm of daily life.

RECAP:
Tangible Ways a Church Might Meet Practical Needs

1. Designate a primary person to communicate with the family and coordinate care.
2. Discover which small acts of kindness would most encourage the family, and then do them.
3. Create specific and well-articulated guidelines that make it easy for the church family to know how to bless the family in need.
4. Create an intentional support plan for ongoing care.

Note

1. http://www.dianedokkokim.com/2013/08/20/just-a-piece-of-paper-in-honor-of-autism-d-day/
2. http://www.latimes.com/nation/la-oe-0407-silk-ring-theory-20130407-story.html#axzz2kF8iBw9U
3. Kara Tippetts and Jill Lynn Buteyn, *Just Show Up: The Dance of Walking Through Suffering Together* (Colorado Springs: David C. Cook, 2015), 11.

Building Community

As we help families affected by disability combat isolation, and as we work together to support their practical needs, we begin to embrace them as vital members of the community. Community is a precious gift. As we draw families into community, we allow them to discover their spiritual gifting and then invite them to express those gifts through service. This includes sharing their own family experience and allowing others to learn from them. It allows families to find a place of belonging—a place to share stories, tears, and laughter.

Authentic community is a reciprocal relationship. Paige, an adult typical sibling, explained to us that the difference between care and community is reciprocity. She acknowledged that there are times when her family needs to take more than it gives, but she wisely noted that you can only build community when there is a commitment from both parties to invest in the relationship.

Families facing chronic illness or disability will benefit from building community with each other, with the church family, and with the broader community.

Building Relationships Within the Disability Community

Typically, people are drawn to others who share similar life experiences, likes, and dislikes. Providing opportunities for families affected by disability to connect with one another allows them fellowship that no one else can provide to them. Within this context they feel known and understood without having to explain themselves or their loved ones. Below are some examples of ways to bring families affected by disability together:

- **Day of pampering:** An event like this is generally geared toward caregivers or mothers. Create a peaceful environment where the attendees can enjoy fellowship and relax. It can be a great idea to include a speaker who can encourage them, pour value into their families, and make them laugh. Consider asking creative members of your church family to create gift bags for each attendee and possibly a few prize baskets as well. You might even recruit massage therapists or pedicurists from the community to come and offer their services for free to bless these weary caregivers. Whether simple or elaborate, you should design the event to help attendees take a deep breath and enjoy a bit of respite from their very challenging everyday lives.

- **Respite events**: Give typical siblings the chance to build relationships with other siblings. Respite events are typically 3 to 4-hour events hosted at a church for children with disabilities and their siblings, giving them a chance to build friendships with others who share a similar life experience. Church volunteers hang out with the children, providing quality care while parents leave campus for 3 to 4 hours of rest. Some parents might choose to take a nap or sit at a coffee shop with a book. Others might run errands that are challenging to do with the kids, exercise, or enjoy a rare meal and conversation with each other or with friends. Many respite events provide fun activities for older siblings that allow them to begin building community. Once siblings have gotten to know each other, some churches will host separate sibling events that deepen those friend-ships and give siblings the opportunity to pro-cess their unique life circumstances. In addition to the online appendices for this book, the Ir-resistible Church book *We've Got This* will walk you through everything you need to know about hosting a successful respite event.

- **Caregiver community group:** Your church might begin a small group for parents and care-givers of special needs children. Caregivers speak the same language and understand each other in a way that no one else can. Providing them with an opportunity to connect and support one another allows them to feel validated and understood. Pro-viding childcare during this time can be critical in allowing parents to attend.

- **Sibling support:** Respite and other family activities allow typical siblings the opportunity to build relationships with other siblings. Once those relationships have been established, they may be open to other sibling support oppor-tunities. Your church could host a sibling sup-port group once or twice a month where typical siblings do fun activities together and talk about life as a sibling with all its spiritual implications. Within these groups it can be helpful to give siblings an opportunity to describe their unique family, recognize shared challenges, learn more about disabilities, and discover how God might be shaping them through their family experiences.

- **Experiences:** Consider asking your church to provide scholarships to some of the families affected by disability within your congregation to attend a Joni and Friends Family Retreat, a camp for individuals with disabilities, or some other experience they might not otherwise have.

Building Relationships Within the Church Community

Everyone wants to belong, regardless of whether they are affected by disability or not. Some families will prioritize building church community over connecting with others like themselves. When families impacted by disability do spend time out in the community, it is most often spent attending activities or programs associated with disability. They are usually excited to be invited to places where their children can mingle with typically developing children and where they can get to know their church family. You can help them build friendships with the church community in many ways, including:

- **Church-wide events:** With any church activity, do your best to include families affected by disability by planning accordingly and offering additional support. For example, if you host a potluck meal at a park you should choose a park that has accessible facilities and equipment. As you and other volunteers prepare food for the event, try to accommodate the dietary needs that the families attending might have. Recruit buddies to attend so that children can play safely while their parents enjoy fellowship. Asking parents and caregivers what types of activities would bless their marriages and children is a great place to start! As you plan events, be sure to intentionally invite families affected by disability so that they know you want them there and have made provisions for them to attend.

- **Small-group participation:** Encourage small groups to invite parents of children with special needs to join. While families impacted by disability can be greatly encouraged through intentional community, typical families will also be blessed as they learn to walk alongside their friends, sharing in their struggles and joys.

- **Invitations to serve:** Families affected by disability do not only want to be served, but they also want to serve and give back. We encourage you to look for opportunities where members of families with disabilities can serve or be in leadership. Each opportunity acknowledges their spiritual gifting and allows them fellowship with other leaders in the church.

Building Relationships Within the Broader Community

The final component of drawing families affected by disability out of isolation is connecting them with the community at large. There are many ways for the church to facilitate this, including:

- **Church networking:** Drawing together community churches with disability ministries can multiply your efforts in serving families needing respite. Your church might even host an event, open to the community, where multiple churches are present, allowing families to see the various ministries and services that are available to support them. When parents witness churches collaborating, it brings them hope and encouragement. Churches that network with one another can coordinate respite and pampering events, allowing families to experience support more frequently. Churches might also come together to host large family events or community outreaches. When parents attend these events, they find fellowship beyond the families in their own church.

- **Weekday involvement:** Families affected by disability have busy lives outside of Sunday morning. Volunteers within your disability ministry can be encouraged to get involved with adaptive recreational and social activities to support these families throughout the week. This also provides an opportunity to represent your church and your disability ministry at community events. Many churches have begun opening their facilities to nonprofits that support the disability community. Hosting a day program or music therapy group at the church not only invites new families to become part of your church, but it also helps families attending your church build relationships with others in the community. It also provides them with an opportunity to proudly share their church family with others.

RECAP:
Tangible Ways a Church Might Facilitate Community Building

1. Offer special family events.
2. Offer respite events.
3. Offer sibling support activities.
4. Offer small groups or Bible studies for parents and caregivers.
5. Provide scholarships to families to attend a family retreat, camp or other event.
6. Collaborate with other churches that have disability ministries to provide stronger support.

7. Encourage buddies to support their students at community disability events.
8. Consider hosting community programs that support the disabled community at your church.

Nurturing the Soul

Spiritual nourishment should be the foundational goal of any church ministry. We believe that this is especially true for any disability ministry, activity, or plan. Our actions are designed to point our friends and their families to the cross and encourage them to consider the eternal blessings of being a Christ follower. Families affected by disability need space to wrestle with their questions about God and their unique challenges. They need to hear repeatedly that their loved one is created in the image of God and that they have value and purpose.

And so, while we endeavor to draw them out of isolation and into true community, we must simultaneously pay careful attention to the nurturing of their souls.

Suffering and disappointment can lead to spiritual confusion. There are many social services that help families combat isolation, provide practical care, and build community. So, what makes the church different from these community programs? Everything we do should be led by the Spirit, guided by our faith, and point to the saving work Christ did for us on the cross.

When a family first encounters disability, they often ask, "Why?" or "How?" The psalms are filled with David's lamenting, showing us that it is OK to share our deepest thoughts and emotions with God. His shoulders are strong and his compassion is great. Facing a long-term disability or the loss of a loved one can cause some families to struggle with reaching out to God, while others refuse to acknowledge Him, wondering how anyone could believe that a loving God exists.

As we discussed earlier, spiritual care should not be about sharing spiritual platitudes, oversimplifying, or pretending to understand. Souls can only be nurtured in environments that are authentic and honest. Trust is built slowly. When scripture is quoted out of context or without compassionate framing, it can have a devastating effect on someone's faith.

We also suggest using great caution when discussing the subject of healing with someone in the throes of a faith crisis. Many families have been wounded by the issue of physical healing. Isaiah 41:10 promises, "Fear not, for I am with you; be not dismayed, for I am your God; I will strengthen, I will help you,

I will uphold you with my righteous hand." Our job is to encourage our hurting friends to turn to God for help. Healing can come in many forms: God may choose to heal someone physically; but his plan may be, instead, to heal their soul and use them through their disability or suffering. The miracle they receive may be the ability to move forward without regret. By putting a limited definition on healing and how God works, we may unintentionally cause others to miss God's goodness.

Do not be discouraged imagining the magnitude of spiritual care—be encouraged! Every time your church makes adaptations that allow an individual with special needs to belong, the rest of the church family is given opportunities to grow in their faith as well. Consider the following ways that your church can support the spiritual growth of families impacted by disability:

- **Worship:** Allowing the entire church family to worship together is a significant step in nurturing the soul of families affected by disability. The Irresistible Church book *Shout for Joy!* is an excellent resource to help you consider ways that our corporate worship experience might be intentionally structured to encourage the faith of our friends who see, hear, move, think, or process differently than others.

- **Community groups:** Including families in community groups is another practical way to nurture their souls. Do your best to communicate clearly with the parents and caregivers whom you serve so that you understand where they would feel most comfortable. Some parents will prefer an intimate small-group setting with other caregivers. Others might prefer spending time with caretakers who are older and further along the road of special needs parenting. Still others may feel that their entire life revolves around disability and would rather be part of a community group that includes families who are not directly impacted by disability. While churches do not typically offer childcare for community group gatherings, families affected by disability would benefit greatly from childcare support that would allow them to grow in faith without their having to find and pay for care.

- **Bible studies:** Bible studies focus on learning the Word together. The group may come to understand each others' lives through sharing prayer requests and praying regularly for each other, but the time together is structured around learning and applying the Bible. These studies should be facilitated by someone comfortable in guiding discussions and knowledgeable enough to answer biblical questions that arise. It is not necessary for this person to have a background in counseling. These groups might study a book of the Bible or use a Bible study series to guide their time together. There are various Bible study books available if the group would like to address the topics of disability and suffering. Study materials should be honest and authentic. Guiding materials should not minimize the struggle or gloss over the pain. In the same way, they should highlight God's faithfulness and his ability to bear our burdens and lighten our load.

- **Support groups:** A support group is a place where people can come to talk about their struggles and seek God's encouragement in the midst of those struggles. Support groups should be safe places with safe people where individuals can be authentic and can vent in a healthy manner. It can be helpful to open a support group with prayer and a short devotional that helps keep a spiritual thread running through the conversations. The leader should encourage participants to share freely and should guide the conversation so that each person can be heard. Authentic and safe support groups can be a critical component of supporting families wearied by the daily stressors of grief and caregiving. Please note that both Bible studies and support groups foster intimate conversation. Because of that, they should be led by someone strong enough to guide the conversation so that no one person monopolizes the discussion and excessive complaining is discouraged.

- **Moms groups:** It is not unusual for the mother of the family to shoulder most of the day-to-day responsibilities of raising a child with special needs. She is often the strategist, researcher, program implementer, and tireless advocate. Most special needs moms feel that it is their job to hold the family unit together. If it falls apart, she may blame herself, feeling like she didn't work hard enough. Moms are generally the family members who are least likely to care for themselves—they don't have many, if any, outlets for self-care or recreation. They are often thinking ahead and carrying the weight of "what if." Providing a place for them to connect with one another and other women in the church can help their daily concerns feel more manageable.

- **Dads groups:** We have repeatedly seen that once special needs dads begin talking about their experiences, they realize how hungry they are for fellowship. Dads have traditionally felt pressure to be the financial provider for their family, struggling with feelings of inadequacy if things fall apart. Often, they feel they do not belong in the caregiving world their wives have created around the children—that they have lost their place or no longer belong. Dads groups are a wonderful avenue for breaking down the walls of stereotypes and encouraging authentic relationships.

The church is the perfect place to affirm and build up dads. This affirmation will undoubtedly begin to reduce the number of broken marriages among the special needs couples in the church. Planned activities for men, like a BBQ, sporting event, or tailgate party, can be a vehicle to start a conversation and a connection. Again, while it is important for special needs dads to connect with one another, it is also beneficial for them to build community with other men in the church. The body of Christ has much to learn from families who faithfully follow Christ in the midst of difficult circumstances.

- **Mentoring relationships:** Caregivers and parents may benefit from spending one-on-one time with someone a bit more experienced or spiritually mature. A mentoring ministry can facilitate this sort of relationship, matching adults who desire this opportunity with mentors of the same sex who are trained to nurture faith and provide friendship. Titus 2 encourages older women to teach younger women and older men to teach younger men to walk in a way that honors God. In some situations, "older" may simply mean "more experienced." When someone has lived long enough to see God's goodness and provision in the midst of disability, they gain a wealth of knowledge. Sharing this knowledge with another who has just begun their walk with disability can be amazingly fruitful for both parties. Again, while it is important to remember that families affected by disability need support, our goal ought to be building reciprocal friendships with them as they have much to offer as well.

The more opportunities we provide for our families to soak in scripture, ask questions, and speak authentically, the more satisfied their souls will be. The more satisfied their souls, the more open they are to God working in their lives and to allowing God to use each family member in the unique ways they have been gifted.

RECAP:
Tangible Ways the Church Might Nurture Souls

1. Provide Sunday support so that the entire family can attend worship services and classes.
2. Consider ways to make your worship services more accessible to every member of the family.
3. Provide community group options for the families you serve.
4. Provide support groups or Bible studies for moms, dads, or couples.
5. Plan men's and women's events to bless parents and caregivers while giving them an opportunity for fellowship.
6. Create a mentoring program

Conclusion

This is a time of great hope. Churches all over the world are opening their hearts and making intentional plans to welcome our friends who have disabilities and their families. Church facilities are being built or upgraded to assure that every person who crosses the threshold has access to every corner of the building and is able to fully participate in every activity of the church. Sunday school programs are being adapted to meet the various learning needs of students of all ages. Buddies are being trained to help their friends participate and build peer relationships. As families affected by disability become integrated into church activities, relationships are built.

Intentional programming naturally leads to opportunities for deeper engagement. But we must recognize that programs are merely a starting point for relationships, and that families affected by disability often go home from programs to lives marked by isolation. Doing life together is a natural outpouring of the Irresistible Church movement. It is a one-step-at-a-time journey. Our prayer is that this book has given you some practical tools for battling isolation, building community, meeting practical needs, and nurturing the souls of the families God sends to your church family. Our prayer is that as God brings families affected by disability into your life, this book will encourage and equip you to build authentic relationships, develop community, and advocate for families in need. And in the process, may you find great joy in doing life together.

"Two are better than one, because they have a good reward for their toil. For if they fall, one will lift up his fellow. But woe to him who is alone when he falls and has not another to lift him up! Again, if two lie together, they keep warm, but how can one keep warm alone? And though a man might prevail against one who is alone, two will withstand him—a threefold cord is not quickly broken."

ECCLESIASTES 4:9-12

Becoming *Irresistible*

Luke 14 commands Christ followers to "Go quickly . . . find the blind, the lame, and the crippled . . . and compel them to come in!" While this sounds inspiring and daunting, exciting and overwhelming, motivating and frightening, all at the same time, what does it actually mean? How do we live and function within the church in such a way that families affected by disability are compelled to walk through our doors to experience the body of Christ?

We can certainly *compel* them by offering programs, ministries, events, and other church activities, but what if the compelling aspect was more about heart, culture, acceptance and embracing? What if our churches were overflowing with the hope of Jesus Christ . . . a hope not simply for those who "fit in" or look the part, but rather a hope to all, including the marginalized, downtrodden and outcast?

Becoming *Irresistible* is more than programs and activities—it is about a transformational work in our hearts . . . first as individuals and then as the body of Christ. *Irresistible* allows us to see each individual as he or she truly is: created in the image of God (Genesis 1:26-27), designed purposely as a masterpiece (Psalm 139:13-14), instilled with purpose, plans and dreams (Jeremiah 29:11), and a truly indispensable member of the kingdom of God (1 Corinthians 12:23). An *Irresistible Church* is an "authentic community built on the hope of Christ that compels people affected by disability to fully belong." It is powerful for a person to know that he or she is fully welcomed and belongs. *Irresistible* captures the heart of the church as it should be—how else do we explain the rapid growth and intense attraction to the church in the book of Acts? The heart of God was embodied through the people of God by the Spirit of God . . . and that is simply *Irresistible*!

The Irresistible Church Series is designed to help not only shape and transform the heart of the church, but also to provide the practical steps and activities to put *flesh* around the *heart* of the church—to help your church become a place for people to fully belong. Thank you for responding to the call to become *Irresistible*. It will not happen overnight, but it will happen. As with all good things, it requires patience and perseverance, determination and dedication, and ultimately an underlying trust in the faithfulness of God. May God bless you on this journey. Be assured that you are not alone—there are many on the path of *Irresistible*.

For more information or to join the community, please visit www.irresistiblechurch.org.

and Friends
INTERNATIONAL DISABILITY CENTER

Joni and Friends was established in 1979 by Joni Eareckson Tada, who at 17 was injured in a diving accident, leaving her a quadriplegic. Since its inception, Joni and Friends has been dedicated to extending the love and message of Christ to people who are affected by disability whether it is the disabled person, a family member, or friend. Our objective is to meet the physical, emotional, and spiritual needs of this group of people in practical ways.

Joni and Friends is committed to recruiting, training, and motivating new generations of people with disabilities to become leaders in their churches and communities. Today, the Joni and Friends International Disability Center serves as the administrative hub for an array of programs which provide outreach to thousands of families affected by disability around the globe. These include two radio programs, an award-winning television series, the Wheels for the World international wheelchair distribution ministry, Family Retreats which provide respite for those with disabilities and their families, Field Services to provide church training along with educational and inspirational resources at a local level, and the Christian Institute on Disability to establish a firm biblical worldview on disability-related issues.

From local neighborhoods to the far reaches of the world, Joni and Friends is striving to demonstrate to people affected by disability, in tangible ways, that God has not abandoned them—he is with them—providing love, hope, and eternal salvation.

Available Now in the Irresistible Church Series

Start with Hello
Introducing Your Church to Special Needs Ministry

Families with special needs often share that they desire two things in their church: accessibility and acceptance. Accessibility to existing structures, programs and people is an imperative. Acceptance with a sense of belonging by the others who also participate in the structures, programs and fellowship of the church is equally necessary. In this simple book you'll learn the five steps to becoming an accessible and accepting church.

To receive first notice of upcoming resources, including teen/adult ministry and community outreach, to learn of upcoming training events, or to access all books and appendices, please sign up at http://irresistiblechurch.org for your free membership.

Other Recommended Resources

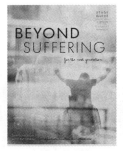

Beyond Suffering Bible

The *Beyond Suffering Bible* by Joni and Friends is the first study Bible made specifically for those who suffer and the people who love them. Uplifting insights from Joni Eareckson Tada and numerous experts and scholars who have experienced suffering in their own lives and will help you move beyond the "why" of suffering to grasp the eternal value God is building into our lives. Special features include: inspiring devotionals, biblical and contemporary profiles, Bible reading plans, connection points and disability ministry resources.

Find out more at http://www.joniandfriends.org/store/category/bibles/

Beyond Suffering® Student Edition

Beyond Suffering for the Next Generation: A Christian View on Disability Ministry will equip young people to consider the issues that affect people with disabilities and their families, and inspire them to action. Students who embrace this study will gain confidence to join a growing, worldwide movement that God is orchestrating to fulfill Luke 14:21-23: "Go out quickly into the streets and alleys of the town and bring in the poor, the crippled, the blind, and the lame.... so that my house will be full."

ISBN: 978-0-9838484-6-2
304 pages · 8.5″ x 11″
Includes CD-ROM

Joni: An Unforgettable Story

In this unforgettable autobiography, Joni reveals each step of her struggle to accept her disability and discover the meaning of her life. The hard-earned truths she discovers and the special ways God reveals his love are testimonies to faith's triumph over hardship and suffering. This new edition includes an afterword, in which Joni talks about the events that have occurred in her life since the book's original publication in 1976, including her marriage and the expansion of her worldwide ministry to families affected by disability.

ISBN: 978-0310240013
205 pages · Paperback

Customizable Resources from the Book

Available for Download at
http://www.irresistiblechurch.org/library

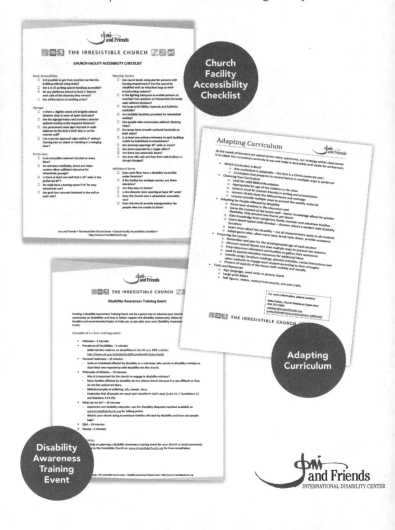